BEDROOMS

BETA-PLUS

BEDROOMS
originally published in Dutch and French
SLAAPKAMERS/CHAMBRES A COUCHER

PUBLISHER
BETA-PLUS sa
Termuninck 3
7850 Enghien
Belgium
Tel : +32 (0)2 395 90 20
Fax : +32 (0)2 395 90 21
Website: www.betaplus.com
E-mail: betaplus@skynet.be

PHOTOGRAPHY
Jo Pauwels a.o. (photography credits p. 200)

LAYOUT
POLYDEM sprl
Nathalie Binart

TRANSLATION
Alexia Aughuet (Dutch to French)
Yvonne Lim and Serena Narain (French to English)

August 2005
ISBN: 907-721-341-4

NEXT
Bedroom designed by
Cy Peys / Partners.

LEFT

A design by Bataille & ibens in a castle renovated by architect Philippe Samyn.

CONTENTS

11 | Preface

14 | Chapter I: TIMELESS BEDROOMS

16   Intimate Atmosphere of an Authentic Farm
20   Timeless Refinement
30   Four Rooms in a Picturesque Villa Next to the Coast
34   Quiet Guest Suite in Brabant Wallon
40   Rural Inspiration
44   Sobriety, Durability, Authenticity

48 | Chapter II: CONTEMPORARY BEDROOMS

50   Craft-Design Tradition
54   A Sea View
60   Calm and Sobriety
66   Natural Materials and Pure Lines
70   A Maritime Ambience
74   Sober Rooms of an Apartment by the Sea
78   A New Sense of Space

84 | CHAPTER III: INSPIRING WORKS BY INTERIOR SPECIALISTS

86   Bedrooms in a Country House in Théoule-sur-Mer
94   Richly Decorated Host Rooms in Grasse
102   Secular Patina
106   Western Inspiration
112   Old and New for Young Couple
116   Timeless Bedrooms
122   Current Rooms in a Rural Domicile
132   Classical and Timeless
136   Tranquility and a Sense of Space
146   Innovation and Tendency
150   Live with Modern Art

154 | CHAPTER IV: HOTEL AND HOST ROOMS

156   Romanticism Inspiration of an Historical Inn
162   Restored honour
172   Secular Castle and Host Rooms with Authenticity
182   Three Host Rooms in a Bed & Breakfast at Antwerp

200 | Photography credits

PREFACE

In 2005, interior designers emphasise considerably on the design and installation of bedrooms as their clients attach large importance to that in the habitation. The current trend is to separate the sleeping area from the shelving and arrangements area, especially when space is not an issue. Rooms arranged in a row, with the dressing area separated, is the most common layout.

Desires for relief and relaxation have not been forgotten: many bedrooms have a living corner with comfortable sofa and television sets.

This publication presents more than 30 modern bedrooms done by renowned architects and interior designers: from the classic to timeless romanticism style to contemporary minimalism.

Despite their great differences, all the works have several common points: the sense of space, harmony of colors, and the passion for materials and natural and warm fabrics.

www.betaplus.com

Next
A project of *Smith
Miller + Hawkinson
Architects.*

CHAPTER 1

TIMELESS BEDROOMS

INTIMATE ATMOSPHERE
OF AN AUTHENTIC FARM

This unpretentious bedroom with a dressing room is the fruit of a recent work in a new farm, done by architect Stéphane Boens for caterer Benoit Dewitte.

The aged ceiling, wrought iron windows and the timber works evoke an intimate atmosphere, which fits marvellously into an authentic rural framework.

TIMELESS REFINEMENT

These two bedrooms are designed by decorator Walda Pairon. We can recognise her distinguishable style from the beautiful use of colours, fabrics and materials in good harmony. Her virtuoso alloy of the old and new is an exquisite refinement: timeless and current.

LEFT AND ABOVE

The doors feature panels made from ancient glass.

The floor parquet extends from the bedroom to the dressing room.

A wooden 17th century "Madonna" statue sits on a small table from the same period.

View of the dressing room seen from the
bedroom. Bed linen with a plaid in cashmere.

LEFT

The dressing room, made entirely of timber, offers
a superb view at the terrace and garden. The mirrors
are concealed inside wardrobe. The oak wood table
dates back to the 19th century.

In the corridor
that leads to
the bathroom,
we notice a
practical space
arrangement.

P. 24-25

In this classic bedroom, Walda Pairon chose to combine objects and furniture with antique values (a walnut wood cabinet, a bench made of sheep bone, goblets and rare carafe in horn, etc), silky fabrics and a pure fitted wool moquette.

NEXT
The master bedroom
has a sober charm.

P. 28-29

The guest room is designed in a Ralph Lauren ambiance, with an antique English bedside table, folded

lampshade, a 19th century office and reproductions.

FOUR ROOMS IN A PICTURESQUE VILLA NEXT TO THE COAST

Dominique Koch has devoted his passion on a picturesque villa inspired by the English style in Knokke-le-Zout: the four bedrooms were repainted and re-furnished with new wall coverings and curtains.

This work illustrates, once again, the sensitivity of this talented designer, orchestrating a subtle harmony of tone and refined motives.

In the bedroom that belongs to the lady of the house: wall papers with shell-shape ornaments and double-layer curtains.

LEFT

The bedroom on the second floor shows influence from the North Sea: Bluish grey tones with stripes.
Ceiling is finished in oak wood.

The guest room is situated directly under the roof. The small windows are furnished with double blinds in Jouy fabric. The custom-made cabinets and bedside tables add to the arrangement of space. Wall lamps are fabricated in good craft-design style.

QUIET GUEST SUITE IN BRABANT WALLON

A young family with four children has renovated an idyllic country house into a spacious and original habitation.

They have created a guest suite under the roof of the annex building, which constitutes a spacious bedroom, a decorated bathroom, dressing room and a small living room.

P. 34 TO 39

The guest suite is furnished with furniture and accessories from Flamant (pouffe, chair, office, telescope, etc), and also features paints by Flamant.

Wall curtains are designed by interior designer De Gryse. The floor is finished with Sisal carpet. Bed is from Vi-Spring. Wall and table lamps are custom-made by Stéphane Donners. The table is from Walter Vilain. The cupboard is made-to-measure by JCB in Spanish wood .

SOBRIETY, DURABILITY, AUTHENTICITY

Dutch designer Alexandra Siebelink plays with old and new materials in an original way to create a serene and current atmosphere. Without superfluous ornaments but with the use of sober and durable materials, she creates true warmth and authenticity.

The design of this bedroom illustrates the philosophy of Alexandra Siebelink well.

CHAPTER II

CONTEMPORARY BEDROOMS

CRAFT-DESIGN TRADITION

The door and windows in an artisanal style in this bedroom are done by E. De Prins, a carpenter who has conserved the meaning of tradition for the past two generations.

Lighting, furniture and all frames are conceived by AlDarchitecten.

The top-slide windows (similar to a guillotine) are fabrications of artisans.

LEFT AND P. 52-53
The panelled doors with retro-style handles are done by E. De Prins.

A SEA VIEW

A house with an interior like a boat, situated at the edge of a lake, is covered with cedar shingles. The lakeside surroundings inspired AlDarchitecten for the design of this interior.

The residence consists of several guest rooms, all conceived in the spirit of freshness, without unnecessary details and a preference of natural materials.

P. 54-59

The exceptional view of the interior attracts all the attention.

CALM AND SOBRIETY

This article presents two recent works by interior designer Philip Simoen.

The trademark of Simoen is easily recognisable in these two projects: a sober composition,
a soothing atmosphere, and a preference for natural and durable materials and fabrics.

P. 60-63

The wall coverings in MDF are whitewashed and varnished. Armchairs from Maxalto (Citterio);
plaids from Lenti and Hermès; bed cover fabric from Zimmer & Rhode.
Carpet from Larsen; bedside lamps from Nogushi; timber blinds from Modo.

Wall skirting and cupboard in old oak. Malear bed cover and Flos wall lamps by Starck.

The office in oak is made-to-measure by Philip Simoen.

Cabinet doors are in painted MDF and oak interior. Tiles in the bathroom are by Dominique Desimpel.

LEFT
In this bedroom in the neighbouring apartment, the wall behind the bed is covered in horizontal strips of oak. Bed cover and curtain are from Malabar. Bedside lamps are from Casamilano.

NATURAL MATERIALS AND PURE LINES

Interior designer Isabelle Bijvoet has created sober lines in this room that is flooded with natural lighting all day. The interior window shutters allow the possibility of either introducing filtered lights or completely blocking out daylight. The laminated cupboard is cleverly inserted into the thickness of the wall, thus integrating perfectly into the layout. The plain oak ceiling with a sober palette of color creates an atmosphere of serenity. All the furniture and accessories in the room were sourced by Isabelle Bijvoet from flea markets.

A MARITIME AMBIENCE

Interior designer Bert Desmet has transformed an original fisherman house into a modern holiday house.

Rooms and dressing rooms in this dwelling are entirely covered in timber: the pine wood wall panels and ceiling strips, together with the floor in oak create an intimate and maritime ambience.

SOBER ROOMS OF
AN APARTMENT BY THE SEA

Interior designer Nathalie Van Reeth wanted to provide this apartment by the sea
with a soothing atmosphere for a family with children.

The apartment constitutes of one volume of space: the kitchen, living and dining areas are found
together in one space.

P. 74-75

The corridor that leads to the rooms is revived by the red tone, yet keeps its soberness thanks to the
filtered lighting and the low level spotlights. The white pivot doors are as high as the rooms. The grey
parquet is found throughout the apartment and form a natural element in contrast with the cupboard
in lacquer MDF. These custom-made cupboards offer additional storage and shelving space. The
rooms are decorated in a sober and bright manner. The window blinds in tissue white and the few accents of colours create a peaceful yet animated ambience.

NEXT

Above the bed: a photo
of Verne (from Items).

A NEW SENSE OF SPACE

The owner of this apartment, a single young man, had the old office place renovated to create a more pleasant ambience to enjoy of the evenings.

As usual, the Brussels design department AXV (Jacques Van Haren and his collaborator Anne Aurélie Defeche) has demolished all the walls demarcating a corridor, a laundry, a toilet and two small bedrooms to create a clear space where the layout is designed to provide a wider perspective. Everything is in white and serves as a reflector for light. The only colours come from the exterior.

P. 78-79

The bed rests on two crossed legs supported at the center, which is not visible when we are standing, thus creating a beautiful impression of a floating bed. Parquet is in waxed bleached oak.

NEXT
The terrace was previously a narrow corridor, which AXV has converted into part of the bedroom by demolishing the lower portion under the existing bays and replacing them with large pivoting frames. Some furniture are painted in MDF while others are made of oak.

P. 82-83

The high pivot doors (with Beau Profil handles in nickel brass from Jacques Van Haren) augment the vertical volume of space to the maximum. When one moves around the central piece of furniture on one side or the other, a clear redefined space articulates the bed, storage and shelving area, and the dressing room in the most humble way.

CHAPTER III

INSPIRING
WORKS
BY INTERIOR
SPECIALISTS

BEDROOMS IN A COUNTRY HOUSE IN THÉOULE-SUR-MER

In this article, Dutch interior designer Bert Quadvlieg presents the bedrooms he has created in a country house in Théoule-sur-Mer.

As usual, he found inspirations in durable materials, vibrant colors and antique furniture to form a harmonious whole.

P. 86 TO 89

The canopy bed in bamboo is designed according to a model of Quadvlieg. Doors to the dressing wardrobe are covered in bamboo and leather.

An office table with "Scagliola" marble incrustation (Italy, 17th century).

P. 90-91

The canopy bed in wrought iron is designed by Quadvlieg. The fabrics are mainly from Ralph Lauren.

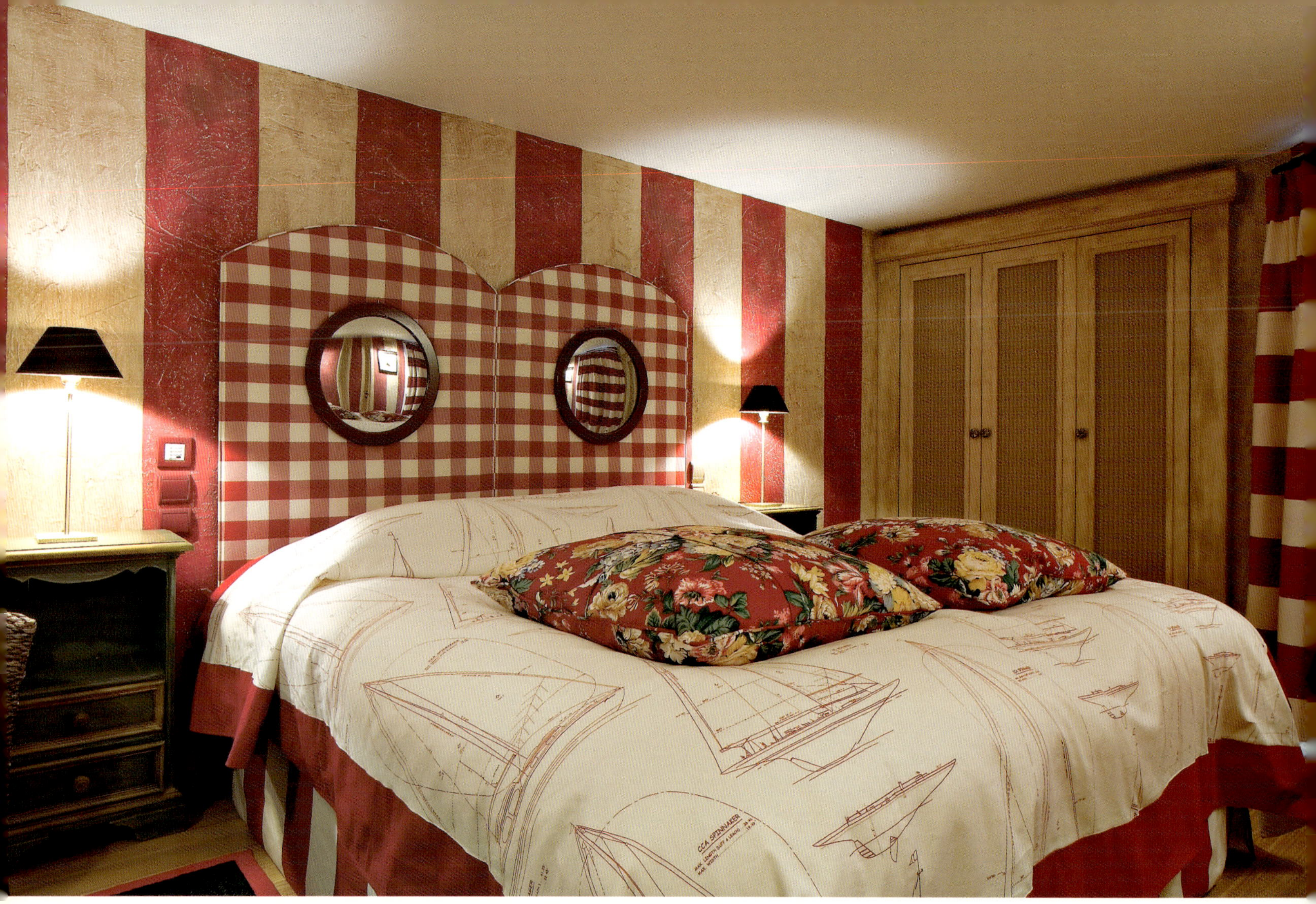

Above

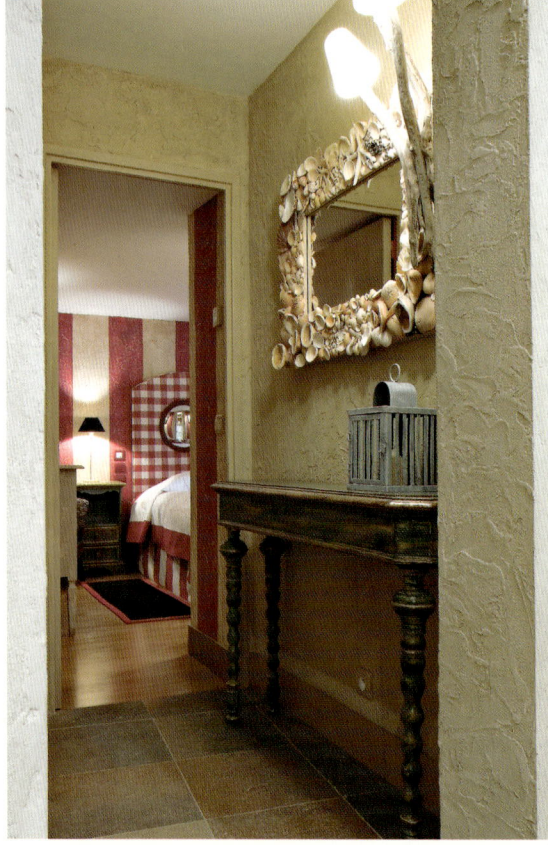

The wall painted with a linear motif is done in several coats. Floor is finished in bamboo.

The mirror frame is made of sea shells from Portugal and Maldives.

The bed canopy and its legs supports are the creations of Quadvlieg. Bright pink unbleached fabric from Ralph Lauren.

RICHLY DECORATED HOST ROOMS IN GRASSE

This is the second article on the work of Bert Quadvlieg (see also P.86-93), who presents here the guest rooms in Grasse.

P. 94 TO 97

The open sandstone chimney is taken from a house that belongs to Helena Rubinstein. The terracotta floor in its original material (around 1950) is the only floor finish preserved in this country house. Wall paper and fabrics are from Ralph Lauren.

P. 98-99

Both the headboard and the sofa bench are dressed up in an authentic kilim (tapestry-woven Turkish rug). A French table from the 18th century is found against the wall. The mosquito net above the bed is made from old grainy sieve. Different varieties of herbs are displayed behind glass frames.

Old wrought iron bed
from Florence. Ceiling in
oak wood.

The canopy bed is made of patinated mahogany timber. Flowery wall paper from
Ralph Lauren. Above the table, Chinese calligraphy texts are framed on the wall.

The decorative headboard in oak wood was originally an ornamental motif above a double door.

The unbleached fabrics are from Italy.

SECULAR PATINA

This article presents two bedrooms and a night hall in a square farm in Wallonie.

Virginie & Odile Dejaegere is responsible for the interior design of this historic farm.

P. 102 TO 105
In this large farm, each room has its own characteristics. Thanks to ancient paint techniques, choice of various antique objects and oak wood secular floor, the bedrooms provide a lived-in timeless atmosphere.

WESTERN INSPIRATION

The attic of an existing dwelling was revamped by Cy Peys / Partners into a room with character and personality that serves as a bedroom and a playing space for the elder son of the owner.

The ludic character and boy's style are accentuated by westernised themes.

P. 106-107

The walls are clad in pine wood panels with a paint that leaves an apparent wood grain. The tinted floor is also in pine wood. Provided with tailor-made comfortable cushions, the play area is arranged underneath the slope of the roof to allow for a clear space at the center of the room. Functional drawers are discreetly incorporated under the play area.

NEXT
View in perspective from the play area towards the bedroom. The wall cupboards that flank the play zone and the rest zone are made-to-measure. They reinforce the space and cohesion of this compartmentalised attic. The cupboards are in vertical strips of timber planks, contrasting the horizontality of the wall that helps to enlarge the room visually.

The office table extends throughout the whole length of the area.

Chairs are from Habitat.

An spare bed is hidden in a large drawer underneath this simple bed.

OLD AND NEW FOR YOUNG COUPLE

Chris van Eldik and Wendy Jansen, the inspiring couple of the store Zon van Duurstede and of the furniture brand, Job, have transformed an old house on a dam into a very pleasant and personalised living environment. The bedrooms of this family with two young children deliver an overall picture: a mix of passion for the old and for the new with distinguished furniture, craft-design, colours, natural materials, etc.

P. 112-113

Furniture from Job Interieur's ancient-style series.

The warm wall colour gives a patina aspect to the wall.

Next
The parents' bedroom is found underneath the roof. Curtains are in pure linen. Bed linen is from Gwendolino and the bed cover from Society. Lamp from Casadisange.

TIMELESS BEDROOMS

Passionate about decoration and interior design, the three Flamant brothers and their team create objects and furniture that seem everlasting.

With a very precise sense of authenticity, Flamant Home Interiors has invented a concept which is simple yet brilliant: the reproduction of old furniture and objects that meet today's need. A mingle of old English styles with the exoticism of the colonies with the Scandinavian or the Provencal style.

Bed from Sleigh and wardrobe painted in white reflects a style of Louis XVI.

LEFT
Canopy bed from Cape Cod in white (160cm x 210cm) and a crossed-legged stool.
Bed linen from Pure Naturel and plaid from Flamant.

The lines however remain very current. Flamant's world is a universe of discreet luxury and an intimate charm.

It offers the perfect combination of individuality, comfort and innovation, as illustrated in this article.

P. 118-119

Flamant always succeeds in combining cultural elements and materials of different styles into a harmonious and timeless whole.

CURRENT ROOMS IN A RURAL DOMICILE

Architect Stany Dietvors has created balanced proportions and volumes in a rural domicile in the Flemish countryside.

The flow between the different spaces is ingeniously constructed: the recently renovated contiguous leisure room and the bedrooms substantially demonstrate this idea.

LEFT AND ABOVE

The transition between the leisure room and the bedroom is unapparent.

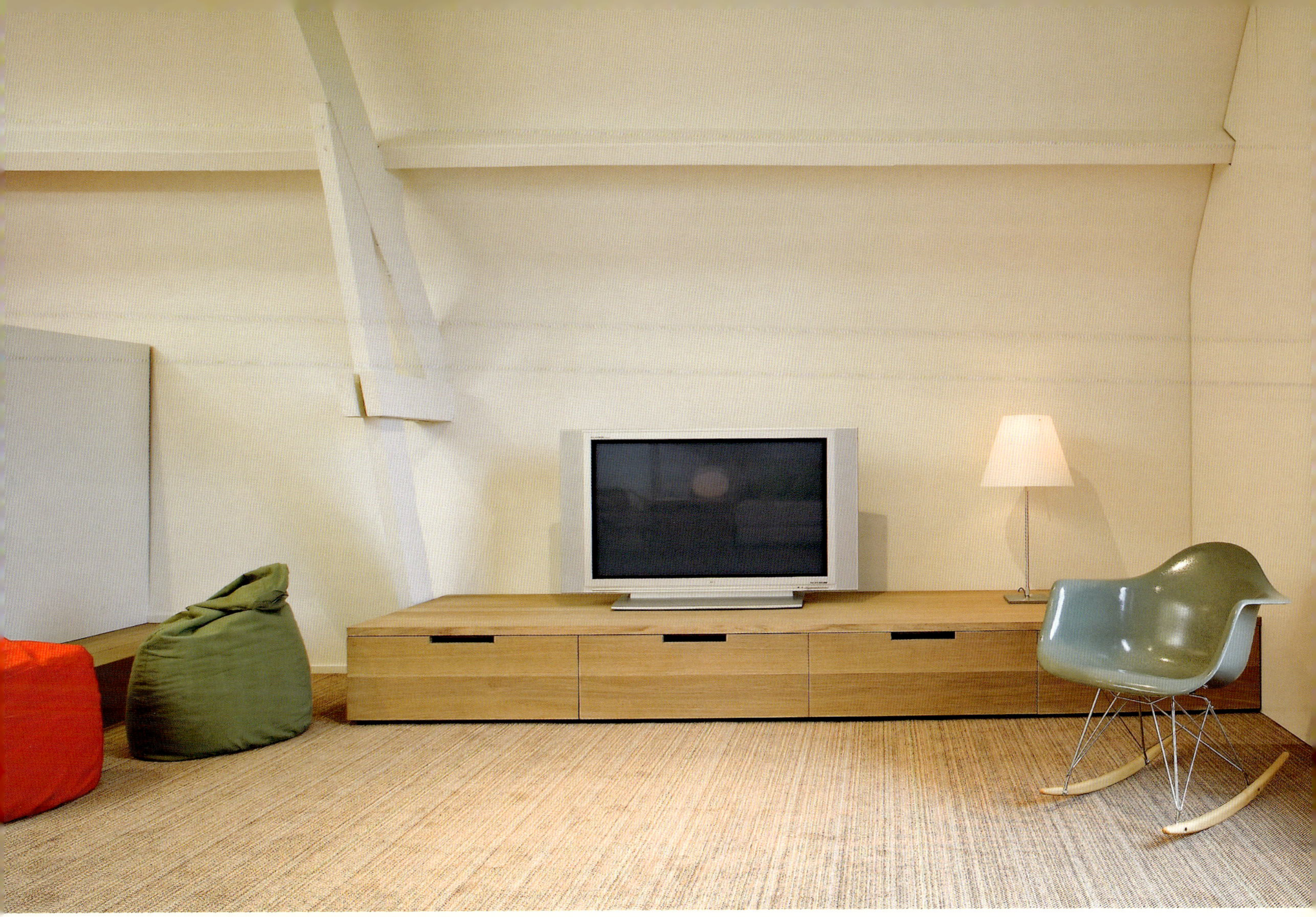

LEFT AND ABOVE

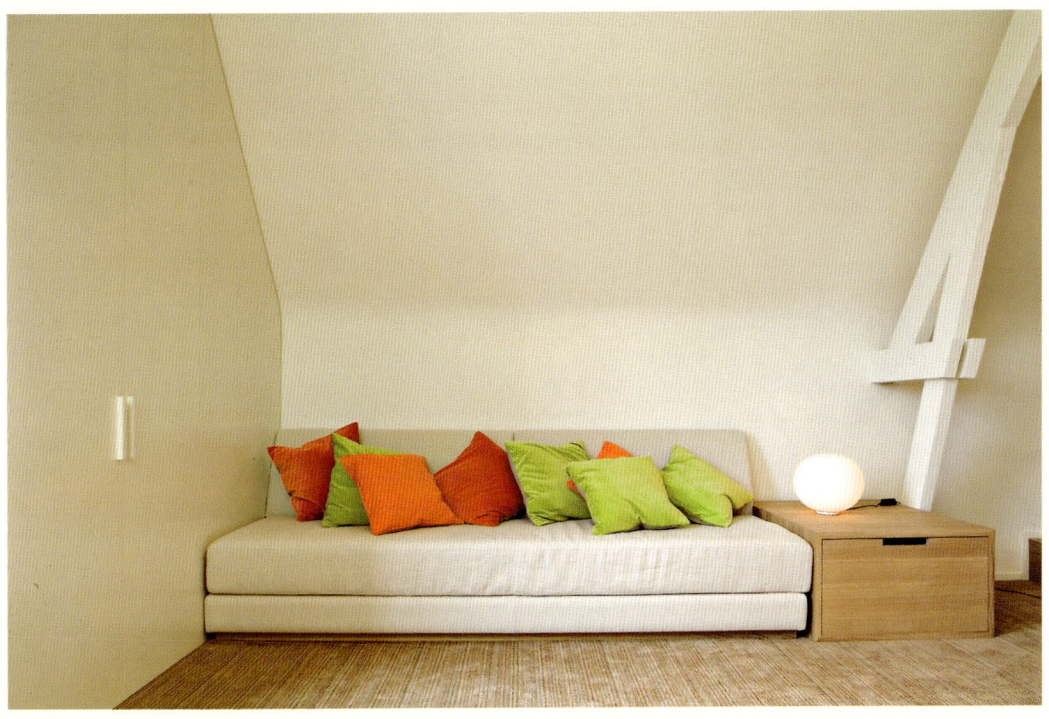

The furniture and cabinets are designed by Borja Veciana Meubelen. The full-height cabinets serve as storage for the toys. The armchair is custom-made by Durlet.

NEXT

The play/leisure room was created by Brussels interior designer Nicolas Dervichian.

CLASSICAL AND TIMELESS

In this house situated on Brussels green belt, the bedrooms are decorated in an accord of old and new: characteristic antique objects and furniture combined with contemporary accents and Orac listello tiles.

Linen window blinds and bleached oak table between retrieved shutters. Bench in Louis XV style with backrest in cane mesh and seat covered with Libeco linen. Plinths and listello moldings from the collection of Orac Décor.

An oak stool in the style of George II under a French painting.

LEFT

Antique mannequin on wooden foot support. The doors feature framings from the collection of Orac Décor.

Working with colours for the walls of the girl's bedroom; a listello tile molding from Orac Axxent marks the separation of the two colours.

LEFT

English tables arranged on both sides of bed. On the background sits a George III chest of drawers in mahogany wood, in between a Napoleon III bench and an armchair of Louis XV style. On its top are different objects and English-style wooden boxes.

TRANQUILITY AND A SENSE OF SPACE

The work of Themenos is traversed by the taste of luxury and well-being.

A bedroom never just remains as what the interior designers have imagined or realised: it evolves with the rest of the house according to the owners' needs and desires.

The rooms, however, remain as intimate and personal spaces whereby the main concepts are designed by the interior designer. Thereafter, they are arranged according to the habitants' lifestyle and way of living.

P. 136 -139

Sleep, play and study in one room while respecting the relevant specifications.

The horizontal lines in scraped oak rejuvenate the whole.

P. 140-143

Themenos has created an ambience of an
authentic suite by integrating the fireplace
with the custom-made furniture.

LEFT AND ABOVE

The unity of materials and the utilisation of colours emanate a sense of tranquility and space.

INNOVATION AND TENDENCY

Smith Miller + Hawkinson is one of the most reputable architectural firms in the Unites States, well-known for both their public projects as well as their individual projects.

Richard Meier has applauded this office for its deep respect for the tradition and modern architecture. This refers especially to the innovation of space and particular attention paid to the site, materials and the human dimension.

This article presents the rooms of one of their individual dwelling projects.

LIVE WITH MODERN ART

Vincent Van Duysen is an architect of international repute due to his remarkable residential buildings
and interiors projects, which is characterised by a mix of austere simplicity,
a near monastic style and warm sensuality.

Owners of this dwelling presented in this article are
passionate amateurs of Modern Art. They have displayed
part of their collection in the rooms.

CHAPTER IV

HOTEL AND HOST ROOMS

ROMANTIC INSPIRATION
OF AN HISTORICAL INN

Situated in the heart of Berges, the Relais Bourgondisch Cruyce emerges from the ordinary with its half-timber panel façade. It is considered as one of the most luxurious hotels in romanticism style in Europe.

The rooms of Bourgondisch Cruyce were recently renovated. Two rooms are presented in this article, both decorated and styled by Brigitte Garnier.

LEFT AND ABOVE

The walls in the rooms are covered in old oak. The bed in oak (same model also available in Mahogany) is an edition of Garnier house. A French console from the 18th century decorates the side wall. The fabrics are from Ralph Lauren.

NEXT
The television and the mini bar are incorporated in the cupboards. The spotlights are from an edition of Jan Van den Hove, found at Garnier House. They come in bronze, nickel and chrome finishes.

P. 160-161

A bright-coloured room under a mansard roof is entirely styled in Ralph Lauren fabrics.

CELEBRATED

In the historical heart of Anvers, two houses were restored to form an exceptional accommodation, the Hotel Julien.

A new layout is introduced to accommodate 11 spacious hotel rooms with superb bathrooms. The open patio forms the link between the two buildings and provides light and space to all the rooms. During the restoration, all important historical elements have been conserved and celebrated. The additions of large windows on the ground floor and staircase permit more cohesion with the interior garden courtyard and make the whole building more open and transparent.

P. 162-163 & 165-167

A timeless and modern symbiosis of antiques, contemporary custom-made elements and furniture design.

LEFT

Ceiling with exposed beams in original paint texture with painted bark in between the beams.

P. 168-171

The made-to-measure cupboard houses a television, DVD player, mini-bar, closet and an office table, with all indirect lighting integrated.

The interior emphasises on sober lines and colours, which accentuates the existing architecture and historical details.

A mix of interesting furniture, custom-made practical elements and restored antique furniture makes each room extremely enthralling.

SECULAR CASTLE AND HOST ROOMS WITH AUTHENTIC DECORATION

Situated in a green polder landscape between Bruges and Damme, the Chateau de Spycker (Castle of Spycker) is five minutes away from Bruges centre. Its history takes us back to the 12th century. However in 1873, it was completely transformed into a typical French style from the end of century. Exterior of the castle displays a typical Flanders-Western neo-renaissance style. The interior is entirely a style of Napoleon III.

The Chateau de Spycker has recently undergone a total restoration due to two antique dealer couples who work in the hotel trade: the Van Haecke and De Clerck families. They have taken precaution to preserve the original architectural elements (plaster mouldings, doors, floor finish, marble floor, etc.). The castle is presently a place to stay, a private showroom for antiques and exclusive fabrics, and at the same time a place to host privileged guests.

P. 172 TO 179

The three host bedrooms in Chateau de Spycker are decorated by Frederik De Clerck with exclusive printed fabrics from Bracquenié and Pierre Frey, taffetas from Métaphores, others from Elsa C., etc, and furniture from their superb antique collections.

The Chateau de Spycker decorates its three host rooms with French printed fabrics based on authentic motifs from the 18th century, painted wood works, thick fleece-lined curtains, etc. The rooms are furnished in distinguished antiques and equipped with exclusive marble-finished bathrooms.

THREE HOST ROOMS IN
A BED & BREAKFAST AT ANTWERP

Slapen enzo is a remarkable address of a
Bed & Breakfast place in Karel Rogierstraat
at Antwerp.

With the help of the design company,
Cotwee, the owners have transformed the
building into an elegant residence of
luxury and comfort.

The three host rooms are designed in
different colour themes and come installed
with a television and hi-fi set.

LEFT AND ABOVE

The Dark Room extends across two stories, which offers much intimacy to the
occupants. The dark colours create a muffled and luxurious atmosphere.

LEFT AND ABOVE

The upper storey and stairs of the duplex Dark Room.

P. 186-189

The White Room inspires calm, intimacy, simplicity and purity.

The Mocca Rocca Room releases a very warm atmosphere.

PHOTOGRAPHY
CREDITS

All photographs : Jo Pauwels, with exception of the following :

P 2, 12-13, 146-153, 196-197:   Jean-Luc Laloux
P 34-39: Patrick Verbeeck